Wounded Warriors

by Ernest R. Laing

Wounded Warriors
by Ernest R. Laing

© 2003 by Ernest R. Laing. All rights reserved
International Standard Book Number: 1-931727-13-9
Library of Congress Control Number: 2003111061

Published by:
Synergy Publishers
Gainesville, Florida 32614 USA
www.synergypublishers.com

Synergy Publishers is a division of Bridge-Logos International Trust, Inc., a not-for-profit corporation, in partnership with Bridge-Logos Publishers.

All Scripture quotations are taken from the New King James Version of the Bible. Copyright © 1982 by Thomas Nelson, Inc. Used by permission.

DEDICATION

*I dedicate this book to my Lord Jesus Christ who
gave me the vision for it and has healed me, a former
wounded warrior. I pray that this book impacts the
lives of many other wounded warriors.*

*Secondly, I dedicate this book to my loving wife,
Christine, who has been a great influence and
encouragement for me in writing what has existed
in my heart for so many years.*

*Lastly, I want to thank Dr. Tom Gill for
capturing the vision and God's heartbeat
for His wounded warriors, and helping
this author put the message in book form.*

TABLE OF
CONTENTS

INTRODUCTION

Have you ever wondered why...

- so many Christians are hurting and battle weary?

- the enemy seems to attack over and over again?

- the church seems powerless to help her wounded?

- there are so many wounded warriors?

To find answers to these important questions, we're going to seek God. We're going to look in God's Word at mighty warriors of the faith who have been wounded, and discover how they became healed and victorious. We'll see that, though wounded in battle, these men and women of God reached out and touched the Lord who was their strength, their power, and their victory.

You, too, will learn how to walk in victory. You'll discover that God really does care about you, and is ready and willing to help you regain your strength so you can fight another day.

You'll also discover that the wounds you've suffered in the past are sources of strength, not areas of weakness. You'll see that God uses every experience of your life to draw you closer to Him so that you can clearly hear His battle plan. Finally, you'll see the end of the battle! You'll see the victory that awaits you as you persevere in Christ.

Take heart, wounded warrior. The Lord has delivered the enemy into your hands.

> *Do not be afraid. Stand still, and see the salvation of the LORD, which He will accomplish for you today. For the Egyptians (enemies) whom you see today, you shall see again no more forever. The LORD will fight for you, and you shall hold your peace.*
> (Exodus 14:13-14 NKJV)

Chapter 1

THE WOUNDED WARRIOR

"I'm tired of all this...stuff! Will it ever end? It seems like I face resistance no matter which way I turn."

Rick was frustrated at his seeming lack of progress in life. At every turn, he faced opposition and had to battle his way through. Nothing came easily; everything had to be fought for.

"Lord. I'm tired. I feel so helpless and broken. Strengthen me, Lord, so I can fight another day."

When armies engage in war, the commanding generals expect casualties to occur. The severity of the casualties depends on many factors, including training and equipment. If the army is improperly trained or poorly equipped, the risk of casualties is much greater than if highly trained and sufficiently equipped.

Likewise, when Christians engage the enemy in battle, the risk of being wounded is very real—especially if they are poorly trained or ill equipped. That Christians will engage in battle is a well-established fact, but how they fare in the battle is another matter.

The Armor of God

The body of Christ is directed to stand in the face of attack and to not faint in the heat of battle. The apostle Paul clearly declared that the battle is not against flesh and blood enemies, but against spiritual hosts of darkness (Eph. 6:12). Paul then proceeded to list the weapons of warfare that Christians should use every day:

> *Therefore take up the whole armor of God, that you may be able to withstand in the evil day, and having done all, to stand. Stand therefore, having girded your waist with truth, having put on the breastplate of righteousness, and having shod your feet with the preparation of the gospel of peace; above all, taking the shield of faith with which you will be able to quench all the fiery darts of the wicked one. And take the helmet of salvation, and the sword of the Spirit, which is the word of God.*
> (Eph. 6:13-17)

God provided the weapons we need to engage and defeat the enemy. The use of God's armor by a skilled Christian warrior minimizes the threat of being wounded. However, many Christians, either through ignorance or prideful rebellion, neglect the armor of God and depend on their own resources. These warriors are at risk and, as we shall see, in need of God's healing touch.

The Wounded Warrior

Let's begin by learning what a Wounded Warrior is. The psalmist said, " For I *am* poor and needy, and my heart is wounded within me" (Psalm 109:22). Have you ever felt like this? Your heart wounded, seemingly broken in two?

The enemy knows that by wounding you, you'll probably be taken out of the battle. He also knows that this battle is part of the war that you are destined to win through Christ! Therefore, the enemy fights with great fervency, seeking to steal from you, to kill you, and to destroy you (John 10:10). He does this with the greatest weapon in his arsenal, deceit. Jesus told the Pharisees:

> You are of your father the devil, and the desires of your father you want to do. He was a murderer from the beginning, and does not stand in the truth, because there is no truth in him. When he speaks a lie, he speaks from his own resources, for he is a liar and the father of it.
>
> (John 8:44)

Have you been wounded and felt like surrendering in the heat of battle? Scripture records how this happened to King Saul: "Now a *certain* man drew a bow at random, and struck the king of Israel between the joints of his armor. So he said to the driver of his chariot, 'Turn around and take me out of the battle, for I am wounded'" (1 Kings 22:34).

Scripture abounds with examples of those who were wounded, either in battle or by thieves. When this is considered in the context of your Christian walk, it's obvious why the enemy wants to disable you. As long as you're a fit and healthy warrior, you are a threat to the forces of darkness.

The Enemy's Plan

When a soldier is killed, it's over—he's dead and that's that. However, if one is wounded, many resources are needed to help that soldier recover. This is one way the enemy of our soul seeks to weaken the body of Christ. He wreaks havoc among the ranks of spiritual warriors, wounding many. Then, others who could be assigned to the front lines must minister behind the lines to those who are wounded.

The enemy tries to steal from you by attacking your joy, your happiness, your finances, and your health. Then, just as with the man rescued by the Samaritan in Luke 10:25ff, the enemy attempts to strip you of everything and leave you half dead.

March To Victory

You don't have to live that way! God promised you the victory in your life as you submit to Him: "submit to God. Resist the devil and he will flee from you" (James 4:7).

We have a Savior, Jesus, who loves us. Jesus died for those who've been wounded and then he arose in power. He is the Commander of the army of the Lord (Josh. 5:14), and

Chief of every battle we are now engaged in or will ever fight in the future.

We'll see in the next chapter how we can be strengthened in the battle by looking at some examples of wounded warriors from the Old Testament. These examples are in God's Word so that we may take heed and learn, but also to lift our hearts up as we are healed of our battle wounds.

Chapter 2

WOUNDED WARRIORS IN THE OLD TESTAMENT

"Just last week I had my car fixed, but now it's broken down again! It's going to cost nearly $500 to fix it. Every time I get a little ahead, something comes along to knock me down again."

"Marti, everyone has problems now and then. Is it really as bad as you think?"

"Yes! Daniel. It's that bad. I've spent nearly all my savings on car repairs, plumbing problems, and a tree that needed to be taken down. It seems like for every three steps forward I take two backward! I don't know how much longer I can hold on."

Does this sound familiar? Almost everyone can relate to Marti's problems in one way or another. Let's look at some other wounded warriors described in the Old Testament and see what God did to help them.

The Shepherd King

King David was a man after God's own heart. From his youth, David pursued God, learning how to worship under the wide expanse of heaven as he tended his father's sheep.

David was chosen by God to become Israel's second king. Though anointed by the prophet Samuel to be king, David honored King Saul until his death. He refused to take the throne until God dealt with Saul.

This decision led to many years of pain and anguish for David, as Saul did his best to kill him. To preserve his life, David was forced to flee into the wilderness. It's there, in the wilderness, that we'll take up his story. Let's see how this mighty warrior and king handled a wounded heart.

At War With the Enemy

David and his mighty men were at war with the Amalekites (1 Sam. 30). They lived in the city of Ziklag, and returning home, found it burned to the ground and their wives and children taken into captivity. Everything was lost! They had no city in which to live and their families were gone as well.

Battle-worn and filled with grief, these mighty warriors lifted their voices and wept till they could weep no more. Then they turned on David.

Talk about being alone! What would David do? What would you do?

"Now David was greatly distressed, for the people spoke of stoning him, because the soul of all the people was grieved, every man for his sons and his daughters..." (1 Sam. 30:6a). David had led these men into battle, but the enemy came while they were out fighting and stole everything from them.

Be Strengthened in the Lord

Have you ever felt like the harder you fight the more you lose, so why bother to fight anymore? Nevertheless, David did something very important when confronted with such tremendous losses: "...David strengthened himself in the LORD his God" (1 Sam. 30:6b).

Take hold of this principle, and your healing will begin. This mighty truth will give you strength, hope and courage to press on despite the obstacles.

David then sought the Lord by asking if he should pursue the enemy. Though David was hurting and angry, he wanted to go after the enemy and take out every one of them, but first he took time to strengthen himself in the Lord. Then he continued to seek the Lord and asked, "Lord, shall I pursue..." (1 Sam. 30:8).

We can learn an important lesson from this experience of David's. When we are hurting and angry, we may feel like the Lord is taking too long, so we charge ahead and try handling the problem our way. But the Scriptures give us a wonderful example to follow in David.

David was hurting. His heart was wounded, not only by his enemies, but by his own men as well. So David, with his wounded heart, strengthened himself in the Lord! He didn't seek a priest first; he sought God first, and then he called for the priest.

If God is touching your heart right now, then stop and run to Him. Strengthen yourself in Him. God is waiting for you to slow down and seek Him so He can tell you, like He did David, "Pursue, for you shall surely overtake *them* and without fail recover *all*" (1 Sam. 30:8).

If you will strengthen yourself in God, in His Anointing, His Power and His Presence, He will give you the direction you need to overtake and recover all that the enemy has stolen from you. God told David to go take back what the enemy had stolen. Likewise, God says the same thing to you. It belongs to you and to the Lord. Go take back your family, your finances, and your health! Go! Take back what the enemy has stolen that was precious to you. Lift up your head for your victory is near!

Share the Bounty

When David went in pursuit of the enemy, 200 of his warriors were so weary they couldn't make it all the way to finish the battle. So David told them to stay at the river and rest, and to guard the supplies.

David and the 400 remaining warriors attacked and defeated the enemy. Reunited with their families, they took the spoils from the enemy and returned to where they had left the 200 men to rest. The men that had fought the last battle were reluctant to share the spoils with those who didn't fight, but David insisted. He declared that none would be left out, and that the entire army would share the victory and the bounty.

This lesson is vital for the church to learn. Too often, a small minority is involved in big projects, and is reluctant to share responsibility, acclaim, praise, etc. However, all in God's army are equal. No warrior is more important than any other. Therefore, God's plan is for everyone to use the gifts and talents God has given them to the best of their ability.

David needed his men to stand guard over their supplies. Likewise, there are soldiers who are assigned to duties in the rear echelon so the front lines can move forward. Their job is just as important, so they must share in the spoils as well.

Fire From Heaven

Elijah was a prophet, a mighty man of God. He was a fearless warrior who single-handedly challenged 400 prophets of the demon god, Baal (1 Kings 18:20-40).

Israel had turned away from Jehovah and followed after Baal, the idol that Queen Jezebel and King Ahab worshiped. So desperate had their idolatry become, that Baal worship was the "official" religion of the land.

God called on Elijah to stand in the gap between Him and the nation of Israel, so that God could again show His mighty power. Therefore, Elijah arranged a demonstration—the prophets of Baal and the prophet of God would each prepare a sacrifice and call for divine fire to consume it. Whichever deity responded was the true God.

All day long, the false prophets of Baal called out to their god to receive the sacrifice. Elijah taunted them, asking if Baal was asleep and unable to hear them.

Finally, near the end of the day, it was Elijah's turn. He prepared his sacrifice and had it soaked in water. Furthermore, he had all the wood for the fire soaked and even dug a trench around the altar and had it filled with water. This is important because the nation was suffering through a tremendous drought that Elijah had earlier called upon the land.

Nevertheless, Elijah knew God. Therefore, he stood and cried out to God to send fire down from heaven to accept the sacrifice. God responded, and the fire that came down not only consumed the sacrifice, but all the wood, the water, and even the dirt where the altar had been! God showed up in mighty power.

Fear Settles In

Elijah then drew his sword and killed all 400 of the prophets of Baal. What a Warrior! But wait! Immediately

Elijah began running for his life from the wicked Queen Jezebel. Her threat to Elijah was real, and he knew it: "Then Jezebel sent a messenger to Elijah, saying, 'So let the gods do *to me*, and more also, if I do not make your life as the life of one of them by tomorrow about this time'" (1 Kings 19:2). Elijah had become a wounded warrior.

Worn and discouraged, Elijah sat down under a tree to pray. He was thoroughly beaten as is reflected in his prayer:

> *And he prayed that he might die, and said, "It is enough! Now, LORD, take my life, for I am no better than my fathers!" Then as he lay and slept under a broom tree, suddenly an angel touched him, and said to him, "Arise and eat."*
>
> (1 Kings 19:4-5)

God sent an angel to strengthen this wounded warrior. By the way, there are plenty of angels at God's disposal to strengthen us when we are tired of running. Nevertheless, even with this encouragement, Elijah was still afraid. Yes. Elijah had a power encounter with God and God won. Yes. Elijah had faith to literally call down fire from heaven. Yes. Elijah knew God and knew what God could and would do. But he also knew what Jezebel could and would do.

You're Not Alone

So Elijah hid in a cave, thinking he was the only one in Israel who had not bowed his knee to Baal. Have you ever felt like you were the only one going through a certain trial? That you're the only one who ever feels like giving up? God told Elijah that he wasn't the only one who was faithful to God. God will do the same for you.

Elijah went on to find a disciple named Elisha who followed after him in great power. When it came time for God to bring his warrior, Elijah, home, Elisha remained at his side until a fiery chariot from heaven came and took him home. Elijah's mantel fell back to the earth and was taken up by Elisha. This great man of God carried on God's work with a double portion of Elijah's anointing.

The Least of the Least of Israel

Gideon was one of the most unlikely warriors in the entire Bible. According to Gideon, his tribe was the least of all of Israel and he was the least of his father's house—his self-image was a mess. According to him, he was the least of all of Israel!

Nevertheless, the Angel of the LORD appeared to Gideon and said something very startling to him: "The LORD *is* with you, you mighty man of valor!" (Judges 6:12). Imagine Gideon's surprise at being called a "mighty man of valor." The Angel went on to tell Gideon, "Go in this might of yours, and you shall save Israel from the hand of the Midianites. Have I not sent you?" (Judges 6:14).

First, God's messenger told Gideon that he was a mighty man of valor, and then that God was sending him to save Israel! What else would anyone need?

A Reluctant Warrior

However, Gideon's response was the same as that of many insecure and wounded Christians. He reminded God that he was of little significance in Israel and his father's house. The problem was, Gideon forgot who was sending him. He went on to obey the Lord and won a great battle with only 300 chosen warriors. Look at the promise given to him by the Lord: "Surely I will be with you, and you shall defeat the Midianites as one man" (Judges 6:16).

This is God's promise to us as well. As His warriors, He calls us together as one man to defeat the enemy.

A Sword in One Hand, A Trowel in the Other

Nehemiah was a cupbearer to the king of Persia, an exile in a land far away from his people. Enemies had besieged Jerusalem and the wall around the city was broken down. When Nehemiah learned about this, he wept and mourned for days, fasting and in prayer before God.

Nehemiah had a heart for God's people that had been wounded and mocked by the enemy. He prayed to the Lord and then went before the king to get permission to go help them. Nehemiah was sent to God's wounded warriors with a battle plan, causing them to "stand together" against the enemy:

> *Every one of the builders had his sword girded at his side as he built. And the one who sounded the trumpet was beside me. Then I said to the nobles,*

the rulers, and the rest of the people, "The work is great and extensive, and we are separated far from one another on the wall. Wherever you hear the sound of the trumpet, rally to us there. <u>Our God will fight for us.</u>" So we labored in the work, and half of the men held the spears from daybreak until the stars appeared.

(Neh. 4:18-21)

God did fight for them as His warriors worked and fought together side by side. God's wounded warriors worked together to defeat the enemy.

Next we'll look at examples of some of God's warriors in the New Testament. We'll discover how the Lord healed their wounds, helping them to help other wounded warriors.

Chapter 3

WOUNDED WARRIORS IN THE NEW TESTAMENT

"Pastor Johnson was right, Marie. The only one we can truly count on is Jesus. Men will let you down, even though they have the best of intentions."

"You're right, Dave. God is our only True Rock. We'll just have to trust Him in this as well."

"Let's pray, Marie, and ask God to strengthen our hearts and heal this terrible hurt. Then I'm sure we can forgive."

Dave and Marie are on the right track. Only God can heal the deep wounds of hurt and betrayal, making it possible to forgive those who've hurt you. No matter how close you get to God, there is always an arrow pointed toward you by the enemy, as he seeks to steal your joy and wound your heart.

Throughout the New Testament we read about the disciples of Jesus who followed close after Him. These men truly loved Jesus and served Him with all their hearts. However, we discover in our study of Scripture, that they were also hurt and wounded as they followed Jesus.

Peter—The Rock

Let's begin by looking at Peter, a man who deeply loved the Lord Jesus. Peter was a fisherman, and was a tough, loud, man's man. As part of his profession, day in and day out, he had to drag heavy nets full of fish. Therefore, Peter was likely very strong and muscular, and we know that he was very outspoken.

On the night of Jesus' betrayal, when the soldiers came to the garden to arrest Him, it was Peter who rose up and cut off the ear of the High Priest's servant. When Peter realized what he had done, he ran away in fear of his life. However, later that night he crept in to where Jesus was being held. Nevertheless, because of his fear he denied Jesus on three separate occasions that night.

After Peter had denied the Lord, he remembered what Jesus had said: Peter would deny Him three times. He was devastated—a hurt, broken and wounded man (John 18:15-27). Peter left the High Priest's compound and wept bitterly, filled with guilt, shame, and grief—his heart was broken. This rough, tough fisherman, this disciple who confessed that Jesus was the Christ, this man who declared his total allegiance to Jesus just a few hours before, was now a wounded warrior.

Jesus' Undying Love

Nevertheless, Jesus loved Peter, even though he had denied Him three times! Jesus loved every one of His Disciples, just as He loves all of us today. He knew Peter was going to become a wounded warrior, just as He knows that you've been wounded. Jesus loves you and wants to heal your wounds.

What a wonderful Jesus we serve. He loved the soldiers that spat on Him and mocked Him; they are among those for whom He died. Jesus also loves those who call Him their Lord and who trust Him to heal the broken places in their lives. Jesus' desire is to mend the broken, wounded heart.

Fear, Hopelessness and Dread

The disciples walked with Jesus for three years. During that time, they witnessed innumerable miracles, saw countless demons cast out, and beheld other mighty acts of God too numerous to mention (John 21:25). These men thought that any day the Lord would smite the Roman army and set up His Kingdom on earth. But then they saw Him arrested, beaten and mocked. They saw Him carry His own cross to Golgotha where He was crucified. They saw the soldiers drive spikes through Jesus' hands and feet, and were horrified when He cried, "It is finished!" and then hung His head and died.

Terrified, the disciples scattered and three days later were huddled in fear of their lives. Thank God the story didn't end there!

Sadly, some of God's children live today as if the story ended in the tomb. However, I declare to you that it didn't end there! In fact, that was the beginning. Likewise, your brokenness and your wounds are not the end of the story.

When the disciples had gathered after Jesus' death, they were broken-hearted. They were hurt and wounded in spirit. They were confused, and wondering why this terrible thing happened.

Let's Go Fishing

Jesus came to where the disciples had gathered and showed them the nail prints in His hands and feet, and the place on His side where He was pierced. Jesus wanted His disciples to know that He was there for them in the midst of their fear and hurt, and that He would always be there for them. He is always there for you and me as well.

The disciples had become discouraged after they saw the Lord crucified and were in danger of separating. Peter told the others that he was going fishing, and invited them along (John 21:3). They were going back to what they had done before Jesus called them. They went fishing for fish, even though Jesus had called them to be fishers of men.

The disciples had gone back to doing what they were comfortable doing before Jesus called them, but it was different now. They labored all night and caught nothing.

When we've been wounded by disappointment or hurt by circumstances seemingly out of our control, our tendency is to turn back to what was comfortable before. The disciples did the same thing. They thought they'd lost Jesus and so they turned back to fishing, but they fished all night and caught nothing. Imagine their discouragement. Jesus was gone, and now they couldn't even catch a fish!

Joy Comes in the Morning

Nevertheless, morning always comes—after the darkest night the sun always rises. "Weeping may endure for a night, but joy *comes* in the morning" (Psalms 30:5).

The disciples saw this played out before their very eyes. "But when the morning had now come, Jesus stood on the shore; yet the disciples did not know that it was Jesus" (John 21:4). Though they didn't recognize Him at first, their promised Hope was there.

When we've been hurt and wounded, we can lose sight of Jesus like the disciples did after His death on the cross. We may have walked daily with the Lord and witnessed His touch in our life. We may have felt His blessing and even heard His voice in our heart, but there are times when the enemy comes bringing pain, heartache and discouragement. Then, despite our familiarity with the Lord, we find ourselves wondering where Jesus has gone.

Jesus Wants to Heal the Broken Heart

Jesus comes to us in the midst of our hurt and suffering. When He does, we may not recognize Him at first, because we are blinded by our hurt, and our wounds and pain block our senses, just like it did the disciples. Remember, they thought Jesus was going to usher in the Kingdom of God by destroying the Romans right on the spot. When things didn't happen the way they thought they would, the disciples became discouraged.

Situations may arise in our lives when we feel like Jesus should do something a particular way. There may even be times when we feel like our prayers have gone unanswered. The disciples felt the same way; they didn't think the Lord could help them. They were seeing with their natural eyes.

When you've been hurt and wounded it often seems like morning will never come. But just as the Lord Jesus came to the disciples in the midst of their discouragement and heartache, so He will come to you. No matter what you're going through, Jesus will never leave you nor forsake you (Josh. 1:5).

The Lord Your Provider

The disciples had fished all night and caught nothing, but Jesus was on the shore calling out to them. He knew they were in need, but still asked them if they had any food (John 21:5). They told Him "No" and so Jesus told them to "cast the net on the right side of the boat and you will find some" (John 21:6).

The Lord loves us and wants to show us where to "cast our nets." It may be as simple as where to attend church, where to pursue your career, or who to have as godly friends.

Jesus showed the disciples that He was their provider, not their previous occupation, and that He truly cared for them. Then Jesus asked them to bring some of the fish they caught so that He could prepare a meal for them. Jesus is the Provider!

Feed My Sheep

After the meal, Jesus asked Peter if he loved Him. Peter answered "Yes" and Jesus told him to "Feed My sheep." Two more times this was repeated, with Jesus telling Peter, "Feed My sheep" and "Tend My lambs" (John 21:15-19).

Jesus wants us to care for each other. Maybe we aren't hurt or wounded, but there are others who need us. Jesus knew that Peter was hurting and He was there to heal his hurts, but He also wanted Peter to minister that same love and healing to others. The Lord Jesus wants you and me, His army, to begin caring for the wounded as well.

The Apostle to the Gentiles

Saul was a religious zealot who thought he was doing God's work by hunting down Christians who were following Jesus. Saul had a heart to serve God, but was going about it the wrong way, so God had to get his attention. On his way to Damascus in search of more Christians to persecute, the Lord literally knocked Saul off of his high horse! Jesus appeared to him and told him to stop persecuting the church and to follow Him. Then Saul was struck with blindness—he couldn't continue going his own direction, but had to be led by someone else (Acts 9:1-9).

While this was happening, another man, Ananias, was being commissioned by God to go lay hands on Saul to heal him. Ananias knew of Saul's reputation, and questioned the Lord about the prudence of going to see him—Saul persecuted Christians, and Ananias was a Christian. However, the Lord assured Ananias that he would be safe, and went on to tell him about how Saul would be greatly used by the Lord (Acts 9:10-16).

Ananias obeyed God, and Saul was healed. Furthermore, Saul went on to become Paul, a mighty Evangelist who won many to the Lord. But what would have happened if Ananias had not obeyed God and refused to minister to Saul, choosing instead to leave him blind?

Have you ever felt like someone deserved what he or she is getting? Have you ever passed someone by because you thought they weren't worthy to be touched by God? This must not be! You don't know if the wounded person you're passing by is another great evangelist like Paul!

Ananias did minister healing to Saul and then he baptized him (Acts 9:17-19). Saul became known as Paul, and through his ministry and writing the entire world has been affected for Jesus. Thousands of souls have been won to the Lord through Paul's ministry, because along the way one of God's servants took the time to minister to a wounded warrior.

The First Martyr

Stephen was one of the first deacons appointed by the apostles to care for the widows and orphans of the new, emerging church. He was a devout servant of the Lord, filled with faith and the Holy Spirit (Acts 6:1-5).

Stephen was also a powerful witness. So powerful, in fact, that he was arrested and taken before the religious court. When Stephen addressed this high court, he preached the message of the Lord without reservation. The religious authorities became enraged, shouting him down and gnashing their teeth at him (Acts 6:8-7:60). They were beyond angry!

The enemy will often gnash at us while we are trying to serve the Lord, and will use others to wound us spiritually and hurt us. However, like Stephen, we must stay focused on Jesus and not the circumstance. Acts 7:55 declares that Stephen, "being full of the Holy Spirit, gazed into heaven and saw the glory of God, and Jesus standing at the right hand of God." By focusing on Jesus, Stephen was able to withstand the worst that sinful men could do to him.

Being full of the Holy Spirit is what makes it possible to remain focused on Jesus. When we are filled with the Spirit of the living God and then are hurt and wounded by others, we too can gaze into Heaven and see Jesus. We can receive His Peace and Love.

Stephen walked into Heaven that day after being stoned by an angry mob. Jesus, his Lord, was there to greet him saying, "Well done, good and faithful servant, enter into the Joy of your Lord!"

Drink From This Deep Well

Other men and women mentioned in the New Testament were wounded and hurting as well. These dear folk were ministered to by Jesus and touched by God's forgiveness, love, and grace.

Jesus once had an encounter with a woman at a well (John 4:7). He sent the disciples into town for food and then sat there, waiting for her to come to Him. Jesus waited in that desert place for her, just like He waits for you in your desert place.

When the woman arrived, she came to draw natural water. However, this woman was hurt and wounded. The people in the city had shunned her and wanted nothing to do with her. She had been married several times, and was even then living with a man outside of marriage. Sadly, the church, like the townspeople, often discards wounded sheep like this woman.

The woman came seeking water but found Jesus. When she had drawn water, Jesus asked her for a drink and then told her about her lifestyle. This woman was immediately convicted of her sin and tried to cover it up by arguing about where to worship. Jesus saw through her response, and offered her forgiveness for all her sin. When the woman left, she was forgiven and cleansed, and many Samaritans believed in the Christ because of her testimony (John 4:10-26, 39).

Thirty-eight Years of Waiting

Every day for thirty-eight years, a man crippled from birth was taken to the pool of Bethesda. Often, an angel would come and stir the waters of the pool, and whoever was first in the water was healed. Patiently, the man waited for his time to come so he could be the first one in the water and be healed.

Jesus walked by the pool one day and saw the crippled man lying there. When He looked upon the man, Jesus asked if he wanted to be made well. The man replied, "Sir, I have no man to put me into the pool when the water is stirred up; but while I am coming, another steps down before me" (John 5:7).

When we've been hurt, we often say to the Lord, "Jesus, everyone else is getting their prayers answered. Why can't I?"

Jesus looked at the crippled man lying by the pool and said, "Rise, take up your bed and walk" (John 5:9). Scripture declares that the man immediately got up and walked after thirty-eight years of being an invalid.

You may not want to wait thirty-eight years to be made whole! Jesus wants you to know that He will come to you, and if you're willing to rise up from whatever you're bound with, He will do the rest! The enemy can't hold you down as long as Jesus is saying: "Rise! Get up! It's time to get up!"

It's Time To Rise Up

You may be hurt and wounded as you read this book, but the Lord Jesus is here for you. Now is the time! Today is the day that you can be healed and rise up in His presence. Jesus is speaking to you today, telling you to "RISE UP." Take up your bed of affliction—the hurt, the wounds—and let the Lord heal you now.

Stop reading now and say a prayer. Let Jesus touch you—He's waiting. Read this prayer out loud:

> *Lord Jesus, touch me right now. I'm hurting. I'm like the crippled man, and I've fallen and can't get up. Please touch me right now, Jesus. I need you! Amen.*

I believe the Lord Jesus touched you as you said that prayer. I rejoice in it with you! Now, continue to walk in your healing.

Next, we'll look at the wounded church and see what the Lord wants to do to restore her.

Chapter 4

THE WOUNDED CHURCH

"So what are you going to do, Larry? Stand or run?"

The words cut like a knife, but Larry knew his friend was right. How did he get into such a mess anyway? All he'd ever wanted to do was pastor a church. Never in his wildest imagination did he think people would turn against him and accuse him of mishandling money—but they did.

"That's really the choice, isn't it?" Larry asked.

"Yes. It's your decision."

"I must remain true to the call. I can't turn away just because things are tough. God will see me through this, Mike. He's never failed me yet."

Those pastor had to make the same tough choice that daily confronts countless men and women in ministry. For a multitude of reasons, some valid and some not, they are faced with the decision to quit or press through the problem.

This isn't a new phenomenon—it's as old as fallen humanity. The enemy of our souls seeks and finds wounded people who will react in unholy ways toward their brothers and sisters in Christ. He does this in his efforts to thwart the plan of God and destroy the testimony of valiant men and women of God, warriors in the battlefield of life.

The disciples of Jesus faced the same question and were forced to make a decision—to follow Jesus or leave Him.

Stay or Leave

During the night, Jesus had come to the disciples walking on the water. They were rowing to the other side of the lake at Jesus' request, but Jesus wasn't with them. He had remained behind. Now, late into the night and facing a storm, here came Jesus to them (John 6:15-21).

The next day, Jesus began to teach the disciples and other followers who were gathered around Him. What started as an ordinary teaching session quickly became a confrontation. Jesus' words were very startling, and the disciples were astonished at what He was saying.

Jesus told those gathered around that He was the bread from Heaven, and that they only followed Him to have their stomachs filled with the bread of this earth. Jesus said that for them to live, they must eat His flesh and drink His blood!

> Whoever eats My flesh and drinks My blood has eternal life, and I will raise him up at the last day. For My flesh is food indeed, and My blood is drink indeed. He who eats My flesh and drinks My blood abides in Me, and I in him.
>
> (John 6:54-56)

The very thought of this repulsed the Pharisees and caused others to turn away from Him, saying: "This is a hard saying; who can understand it?" (John 6:60). Many followers decided to leave Jesus, and turned back to their old ways of life. The twelve were faced with a decision as well. Should they stay or leave?

Then Jesus asked His disciples if they wanted to leave too, but Peter said, "Lord to whom shall we go? You have the words of eternal life...we have come to believe and know that you are the Christ, the Son of the living God" (John 6:68-69).

Jesus does have the words of eternal life. We can rest and have peace in our lives when we stand on the truth that Jesus is the Son of the living God. We can know that Jesus is working on our behalf, and that all things work together for good for those who love Him and believe in Him.

Minister Healing to One Another

There are many hurt and wounded soldiers in the church today. Newspapers and prime-time television hawk the stories about once mighty men of God who have fallen into sexual sin, or schemed to take money using the name of the Lord. Though these leaders were wrong for doing such things, Jesus still wants to heal and restore them. Jesus desires to heal all of His wounded warriors and to bring healing to His body, the church.

The Lord wants us to care for and minister to one another. To facilitate this, many churches today are emphasizing cell groups. These are small groups of Christians who meet in each other's homes. These informal settings enable believers and non-believers alike to get to know the Lord and each other better, while helping to meet one another's needs.

Jesus modeled this as recorded in John 13:1-17, by washing the disciples' feet. Peter didn't want Jesus to wash his feet, saying, "'You shall never wash my feet!' Jesus answered him, 'If I do not wash you, you have no part with Me'" (John 13:8). Peter then told Jesus to wash not only his feet, but also his hands and his head.

Jesus knows that you are hurting and He wants to wash your feet and cleanse you. However, like Peter, you must receive the gift of the Lord. Cry out to Jesus and say, "Yes, Lord. Wash me and cleanse me from my head to my feet."

The church must apprehend this principle. Jesus was very clear in what He told the disciples:

> *If I then, your Lord and Teacher, have washed*
> *your feet, you also ought to wash one another's*
> *feet. <u>For I have given you an example, that you</u>*
> *<u>should do as I have done to you.</u>*
>
> (John 13:14-15)

This teaching is key for the wounded church. We must tend to our wounded instead of letting them leave thinking that nobody cares for them.

Love One Another

When Jesus was being crucified, while hanging on the cross, He looked down and saw His mother. John, Jesus' beloved disciple, was standing by comforting her through this terrible and tragic event. Jesus looked at John and gave him charge over His mother. Because Jesus was the oldest son, it was His responsibility to look after His mother.

> *When Jesus therefore saw His mother, and the dis-*
> *ciple whom He loved standing by, He said to His*
> *mother, "Woman, behold your son!" Then He said*
> *to the disciple, "Behold your mother!" And from*
> *that hour that disciple took her to his own home.*
>
> (John 19:26-27)

This is a primary example of the body of Christ ministering to each other. It's helping those who are fellow believers and servants of the Lord. If only the Church would apply this as a lifestyle, then churches splitting would be much less common! We must tend to our wounded. We must pray for them and then put feet to those prayers by actually reaching out to meet their needs. We must lift them up, and hold up their hands so they are able to fight another day and win the battle. Our enemy wants to scatter God's army. He wants us to be separated so we can be destroyed.

A very common tactic of war is to separate a unit of soldiers from the main company and then attack. This is exactly what our enemy wants to do to the church today. He wants to separate believers and cause division, and then move in for the kill. However, we can stop this process by learning how to love and care for one another.

It's not too late, so let's start now—today! Let's band together in God's army and learn how to love one another.

Next chapter, we will look at a battlefield scene, and a vision the Lord gave me concerning His church.

Chapter 5

THE BATTLEFIELD VISION

This chapter is the heart of the book, so please pray as you read it. Ask the Lord what He would have you do.

During the year 1988, just after returning home from preaching a revival in Canada, I was sitting in my family room. It was late in the afternoon, and I was alone, praying for two brothers in Christ. They were mighty warriors for God, and both had seemingly fallen into sin.

One brother had a Christian empire, a retreat center for Christians, complete with a television studio, hotels and restaurants—all in a Christian atmosphere. I know, because I had a lifetime membership and had been on his television program. When I learned what this brother had done, my heart was broken. Weeping, I held him up in prayer.

Then I thought of another evangelist whose sin had been exposed. Like the first brother, he had to step down as well. This man of God had led millions to Christ in stadiums and conference halls around the world. He would weep as he ministered and played his music, and when he gave an altar call, thousands would respond to find Jesus as their Savior. Nevertheless, he had fallen into sin.

So on this afternoon, I was alone praying for these men. I can't tell you exactly how the next event happened, except that the Lord took me to a battlefield to show me something. What follows is the vision that I saw on that afternoon. This vision lasted for nearly an hour, and it has radically marked my life.

The Vision

Suddenly, I found myself high up in the night sky, above a battlefield scene in a valley below. An angel was standing to my left. as I was, he was watching the battle rage below. All of a sudden, we began to move down toward the battlefield in the valley. We seemed to be moving toward the rear lines of this great battlefield.

I noticed soldiers dressed for battle in helmets with breastplates, swords, and shields. When I looked a second time, I saw that most of these soldiers were wounded. Some were kneeling in prayer with their helmets askew. Some were lying down, propped up on one elbow with holes in their breastplates, and blood was spilling out from their wounds. Some were kneeling with their head in their hands, weeping. A few soldiers were standing and just staring, as if in a trance. Many had only half of a sword.

I turned to the angel and asked where their help and their backup were. The angel didn't answer me. Instead, we moved on through these wounded soldiers towards the very middle of this great battlefield scene.

I noticed that in the middle of this battlefield, there were no soldiers. As I looked, I saw weapons that looked almost new just lying there in the dirt and dust! I saw swords scattered here and there, shields laying in the dirt, and helmets all over the place. Where were the warriors? No wonder those soldiers at the rear of the battlefield were wounded!

I became angry, so I turned to the angel and asked, "Where are the soldiers? Did they just run away from the battle? Are they afraid of the enemy?" Still, there was no answer from the angel, just silence.

We began to move again, and I knew that we were headed toward the frontlines. Drawing nearer, I could hear the curses and screams of the enemy. They were swearing and mocking as we drew nearer to the front.

Then I saw them. Standing on the frontlines in the face of the enemy were a few soldiers. They were standing in place, swords drawn and held high. Though their armor was worn, it was still in place. As we drew closer, I saw their faces smudged with dirt. Then, I looked at their eyes. Their gaze seemed to be fixed upon something beyond the front lines, beyond the battlefield. They were almost ignoring the enemy's mocking and cursing.

I was about to ask the angel what was going on, when suddenly I saw what the soldiers were looking at. I fell on my knees next to the angel, for beyond the battlefield in the night sky and amidst the stars, was a massive white horse pawing with his front hoof as if he were ready to run. I saw a golden bridle on the horse's mane and a hand holding the bridle. Then I saw a nail print on the wrist and I looked up into the face of our Lord and Savior, Jesus Christ—our soon coming King.

As I looked at Jesus, I saw a tear running down His cheek. This is what He said to me that afternoon:

> *Tell my wounded warriors to hold on, I'm coming! Hold on! I'm coming! I'm going to mount up and ride into the battle. I'm going to ride to the back lines and dismount and hold those wounded warriors. As I hold them, I'm going to pour oil and wine into their open wounds. I'll heal them with my love and power. I'll seal all the holes in their armor, and I'll raise them. Together we will defeat the enemy!*
>
> *Son, those weapons and the armor you saw in the middle of the battlefield belong to my precious wounded warriors who have left the battle because of discouragement, disappointment, heartache and fear. They have walked away just like the prodigal son. Tell them to come home. Tell them that just as the prodigal son's father looked down the road day*

*after day and longed for him to come home, so have
I been looking and waiting for them to come back,
so that I may place the ring of my authority upon
their finger. I will heal their wounds. I will never
forsake them. I will fit their armor upon them and
will lead them into victory.*

*Those few soldiers that you saw at the front
lines are my warriors who have stood and held the
enemy back, and kept their eyes on me. Tell them
that I will ride to the front lines and join them. I will
empower them and anoint them for service. Then,
together we will raise up others who have been
wounded to fight again and be victorious.*

When the Lord finished showing me this vision, I wrote
it down. Then He told me to go to the churches and share
it. He also told me to write this book to all the wounded
warriors.

The final chapter is about the final battle, and the joy of
knowing that after the battle is won, we will never be
wounded again.

Chapter 6

THE FINAL BATTLE

"Mick. I've finally beaten it! I'm not going to be plagued any more by the enemy in that area of my life! Thank God!"

"I'm really excited, Bob. I know that you've struggled with it for years—and put up with a lot of grief from others about it as well."

"It's over. The battle's been won and I'm walking in victory."

The struggle that Bob finally won has been a weak spot in his armor for years. Regularly, the enemy would take advantage of this weakness to knock Bob out of the battle. However, he learned that God's will is for him to succeed and not fail. He also learned that the Holy Spirit gives him the power to overcome.

You, too, have the power to overcome. This chapter is critical for every wounded warrior who needs to be encouraged and strengthened.

We've read about how the warriors of God have been wounded in battle throughout the ages. We've seen examples from both the Old and New Testaments of the Bible, and discussed how these wounded warriors comprise the wounded church. We've also seen the mandate given to me by the Lord Himself to spread the word about His desire to heal the wounded and lead them into victory.

Now, we'll witness the final battle and rejoice at the outcome as these remaining questions are answered:

- What makes the battles we face as Christians worthwhile?

- How can we be victorious and know that there is a great light at the end of the tunnel?

- Is it possible to defeat the enemy of our souls, right now, today, or must we wait until Jesus returns?

The Art of War

Let's begin by examining the art of war and what God's Word says. Warriors are usually wounded in some kind of warfare, but as part of God's army, we can follow His strategic battle plan.

God has a faultless battle plan. He's given us everything we need to defeat the enemy's attack, including the weapons! We must fight the good fight. Consider these Scriptures:

> *This charge I commit to you…according to the prophecies previously made concerning…that by them you may wage the good warfare…*
> (1 Tim. 1:18)

> *When you go out to battle against your enemies, and see horses and chariots and people more numerous than you, do not be afraid of them; for the LORD your God is with you.*
> (Deut. 20:1)

> *For the weapons of our warfare are not carnal but mighty in God for pulling down strongholds…*
> (2 Cor. 10:4)

If you get too busy with the things of this world and neglect praying and reading God's Word, you'll grow weary and let your guard down. God's Word is your Warfare Manual, so READ IT! Only by communing with Him in prayer will you hear the latest orders and strategy for the battle, so PRAY! The enemy desires to attack you when you're down. Therefore, as a soldier in God's Army, you must be alert and ready—prayed up and studied up—so that you'll have what you need for the battle. Only then will you defeat the enemy and move forward in God's plan for your life.

With that in mind, you can understand why God said, "No one engaged in warfare entangles himself with the affairs of this life, that he may please him who enlisted him as a soldier" (2 Tim. 2:4).

God will teach you how to wage war, because He is a mighty warrior!

> *He teaches my hands to make war, so that my arms can bend a bow of bronze.*
>
> (2 Sam. 22:35)

> *The LORD is a man of war; The LORD is His name.*
>
> (Exodus 15:3)

The War is Won

Let's look ahead to the final battle. Let's see how the stage is set and how God's warriors will play a part in this last engagement. Remember, the same wounded warriors that God has touched and healed fill a vital role in the crushing defeat of the enemy:

> *And war broke out in heaven: Michael and his angels fought with the dragon; and the dragon and his angels fought, but they did not prevail, nor was a place found for them in heaven any longer. So the great dragon was cast out, that serpent of old, called the Devil and Satan, who deceives the whole world; he was cast to the earth, and his angels were cast out with him.*
>
> (Rev. 12:7-9)

And they overcame him by the blood of the Lamb and by the word of their testimony, and they did not love their lives to the death.

(Rev. 12:11)

These are powerful verses for every warrior of God. The blood of Jesus and the word of our testimony are the powerful weapons we'll use to overcome the enemy. As we focus our eyes on Jesus, the author and finisher of our faith, we'll be willing to lay down our lives, knowing that the enemy can't destroy us. The enemy may damage our bodies, but God has our lives in His mighty hand!

You Must Have the Testimony of Jesus

The Word of God clearly reveals that there is a real enemy and a real battle to fight: "And the dragon was enraged with the woman, and he went to make war with the rest of her offspring, who keep the commandments of God and have the testimony of Jesus Christ" (Rev. 12:17).

If you don't have the testimony of Jesus, you can receive it right now by opening your heart to the Lord Jesus Christ. Receive Him as your personal Savior by praying this simple prayer:

Lord Jesus. Forgive my sins. Come into my heart and be my Lord and Savior. I give my life to You, and I want You to live through me from this day forward. In Jesus Name. Amen.

If you just prayed this prayer, you are now one of God's mighty warriors! Welcome to the family: "as many as received Him, to them He gave the right to become children of God, to those who believe in His name" (John 1:12).

God's warriors are those who've confessed that Jesus is their Lord and Savior. Together with Jesus, we'll fight the enemy, those who "make war with the Lamb, and the Lamb will overcome them, for He is Lord of lords and King of kings; and those who are with Him are called, chosen, and faithful" (Rev. 17:14).

Though once wounded, every one of God's mighty warriors will be present at the fulfillment of the following Scriptures:

> *Now I saw heaven opened, and behold, a white horse. And He who sat on him was called Faithful and True, and in righteousness He judges and makes war. His eyes were like a flame of fire, and on His head were many crowns. He had a name written that no one knew except Himself. He was clothed with a robe dipped in blood, and His name is called The Word of God. And the armies in heaven, clothed in fine linen, white and clean, followed Him on white horses. Now out of His mouth goes a sharp sword, that with it He should strike the nations. And He Himself will rule them with a rod of iron. He Himself treads the winepress of the fierceness and wrath of Almighty God. And He has on His robe and on His thigh a name*

written: KING OF KINGS AND LORD OF LORDS.

And I saw the beast, the kings of the earth, and their armies, gathered together to make war against Him who sat on the horse and against His army.

Then I saw an angel coming down from heaven, having the key to the bottomless pit and a great chain in his hand. He laid hold of the dragon, that serpent of old, who is the Devil and Satan, and bound him for a thousand years; and he cast him into the bottomless pit, and shut him up, and set a seal on him, so that he should deceive the nations no more till the thousand years were finished. But after these things he must be released for a little while.

(Rev. 19:11-16, 19; 20:1-3)

Our Glorious Future

The last two chapters in the Bible, Revelation 20 & 21, reveal our glorious future. We are told about our eternal home with the Lord and that the war is over! It's been won, so there are no more battles, no more pain, no more broken hearts, and all eternity to spend with our Lord and Savior Jesus Christ!

My prayer is that this book has helped those of you who've been wounded to receive God's healing. I pray that you'll take up the battle again, and begin to walk in victory over the evil one. I also pray for your families that the Lord will touch and heal them as well.

May God be with you and bless you. May the Commander-In-Chief of this mighty army of God, our Lord and Savior, Jesus Christ, give you strength and victory.

Even so, come quickly, Lord Jesus. AMEN!

ABOUT THE AUTHOR

R ev. Ernest R. Laing is an ordained minister who holds black belts in two styles of martial arts. He served as an officer in the United States Army, 19th Special Forces, from 1970 to 1978 in the 5th Green Beret Division.

The training for war Rev. Ernie received in his military service has been useful in helping him understand the warfare that believers experience in the spiritual realm. The Lord has shown him how to use spiritual weapons to combat the enemy, often through the occasions of his own wounding. Through this, the Lord has given him a mandate to help others who have been wounded in battle.

Rev. Ernie speaks to churches and leaders across the nation with a powerful message of restoration to those hurt and wounded. During the meetings, the presence of God is often so strong that many of God's wounded soldiers are healed. Rev. Ernie has dedicated his life to help those who are hurt and wounded.

Rev. Ernie Laing may reached at:

America Back to God Ministries
56097 Birkdale Drive
Macomb, Michigan 48042